474

HANDBOOKS OF EUROPEAN NATIONAL DANCES

GENERAL EDITOR

VIOLET ALFORD

DANCES OF IRELAND

Plate 1   Galway and Connemara Shawls and Munster Cloak

DANCES of IRELAND

PEADAR AND GERALD O'RAFFERTY

PUBLISHED

UNDER THE AUSPICES OF

THE ROYAL ACADEMY OF DANCING

AND THE

LING PHYSICAL EDUCATION ASSOCIATION

LONDON

MAX PARRISH & COMPANY

FIRST PUBLISHED IN 1953 BY
MAX PARRISH AND CO LIMITED
55 QUEEN ANNE STREET LONDON W.1

ILLUSTRATED BY
MARY FAIRCLOUGH
AFTER EARLY
NINETEENTH-CENTURY
IRISH PRINTS AND DRAWINGS
EDITED BY
YVONNE MOYSE, M.A.

PRINTED IN GREAT BRITAIN BY
BILLING AND SONS LTD GUILDFORD AND ESHER
MUSIC PHOTO-SET BY
HALSTAN AND CO LTD AMERSHAM

CONTENTS

✣✣✣

Illustrations in Colour, pages 2, 12, 29, 39
Map of Ireland, page 6

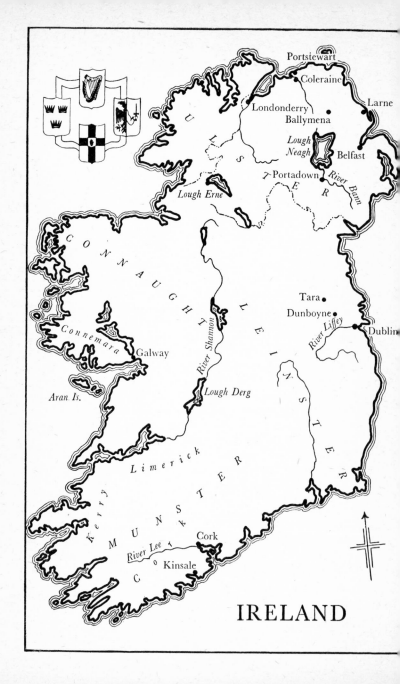

IRELAND

INTRODUCTION

> *Ich am of Irlaunde*
> *Ant of the holy londe*
> *of Irlande.*
> *Gode Sire, pray ich the,*
> *For of saynte Charité,*
> *Come ant daunce wyth me*
> *In Irlaunde.*
>
> Anon. *c.* 1300

No book has yet been written dealing exclusively with the history of Irish dancing and, except for an essay or two, only scattered, often contradictory, allusions to the subject are to be found. The disturbed state of the country during and after the Tudor wars, together with the ordinances forbidding everything Irish, including the Irish language, are responsible for the decline in the peaceful arts and for the gap in both oral and written records. Yet, before the wars engulfed the country, Irish music and dancing were much admired and had permeated English life to an extent now difficult to appreciate. It is indeed mostly from English sources that we learn something of the National dances of Ireland. If our own literature told us more, we might be able to extend to our dancing the tribute of the scholastic divine John Major (1469–1550) to our music *'Hibernenses . . . qui in illa arte praecipui sunt'.**

The fourteenth-century poem which opens this short study is probably the earliest known reference to dancing in Ireland, for such well-known investigators as Joyce, O'Curry and Stokes have searched Gaelic literature in vain.

The next reference is found in a letter written by Sir Henry Sidney (1569) to Queen Elizabeth, although there

* Flood & W. H. Grattan: *History of Irish Music,* 1905.

is a theory that Sir Anthony St. Leger, when Lord Deputy
of Ireland (1540), saw the Round which now goes by his
name and brought it back to England with him.* The
1569 letter speaks specifically and enthusiastically of the
Irish Jigs danced by the ladies of Galway who, says Sidney,
'are very beautiful, magnificently dressed and first class
dancers'.† Later we learn that, in the time of Charles II,
in Dublin 'graceful gentlemen were wont to dance with
the fair ladies of the Court in the fashion of the Hey and
the Fada'.‡

The widespread Hey is nowadays, in Ireland, properly
applied to a movement, such as the 'Ladies' Figure' in
The High Caul Cap, while the Fada means the Rinnce
Fada, known also as the Fading.§ This, Flood considered,
was the ancestor of the Faddy or Furry dance of Cornwall,
where a Celtic tongue was in use until the eighteenth
century. He also held that the Country dance, Trenchmore,§ was an anglicised version of Rinnce Mor (the
Great Dance) or Rinnce Fada (the Long Dance). Certain
it is that Irish music and dancing were much in vogue in
England during the last years of Elizabeth's reign. Even
the critical Fynes Moryson‖ accorded them his approbation
saying 'They [the Irish] delight much in dancing, using no
arts of slow Measures or lofty Galliards, but only Country
dances of which they have some pleasant to behold such
as Bulrudery and The Whip of Dunboyne, and they dance

* But this would be much disputed, bearing as it does such eminently
English characteristics in both dance and tune. Sellenger's Round was
an English Maypole dance at one period of its long life. Playford's
Dancing Master gives it once as a Longways and Sir John Hawkins
(*General History of Music*, 1766) considered it 'the oldest English Country
dance now extant', which Chappell denies. *General Editor*.

† Flood & W. H. Grattan, *op. cit.*

‡ O'Keefe & O'Brian: *Handbook of Irish Dances*, 1902.

§ 'Trenchmore of forty miles long' 1627. See Chappell's *Popular
Music of the Olden Times*, vol. I, pp. 82, 234.

‖ Fynes Moryson (1566–1630): *Manners and Customs of the Irish.*

commonly about a fire in the midst of a room holding withes in their hands and by certain strains drawing one another into the fire.'

✤ THE RINNCE FADA AND THE HEY ✤

If any claim to antiquity be made for Irish dancing it must be based on these two dances. The authors feel that there is a connection between the ancient forms of fire-worship common in Ireland and the original forms of the Rinnce Fada and the Hey. Fire ceremonies were performed at Beltane, on the Eve of May Day, one of the great Celtic feasts, when amongst other acts the cattle were driven between two fires to be purified by the smoke and preserved from disease during the coming year. One may imagine the participants moving on either side of the line of beasts, urging them between the fires or, alternatively, towards the smoke of either fire, and as nothing dies harder than tradition, it is easy to see how such ceremonial line-movements might develop into a dance and continue long after their significance was forgotten.

Relics of this fire ritual remained right into the eighteenth century in some parts of Ireland. It was during a fire festival on May Eve that the young lady, who wrote as Elizabeth Charlotte, saw the 'White Horse' rearing and plunging in the flickering light of the flames. Hers is a vivid description of this Spring animal-divinity which we know in a similar shape in the Mari Lwyd in South Wales and in a very different form at Padstow, Cornwall, at Minehead, Somerset, and at other places in England, not to mention innumerable European examples.

The Irish 'White Horse', like the present-day Welsh one, was made of a real horse skull fixed to a pole, the man carrying it being shrouded by a white sheet, but his ritual season was May whilst the Welsh horse commemorates a Midwinter ritual.

9

Fynes Moryson's dance 'about a fire' may have been some racial memory that dancing was connected with fires, or even took place round a fire built in the centre of a room, as in most early dwellings.

The Rinnce Fada was a popular dance and those who danced it were 'much addicted on holidays, with the bagpipe, Irish harps and Jews' harps to dance after their country fashion, that is the *long dance*, one after another, of all conditions, masters, mistresses and servants'.*

An old description of the dance was: 'Three abreast, each holding the ends of a white handkerchief, moved a few paces forward to slow music, the rest following in pairs, a white handkerchief held between them. Then the dance began. The music changed to a brisk time, the dancers passed with a quick step under the handkerchiefs of the three in front, wheeled round in semi-circles and formed a variety of pleasing evolutions interspersed with *entrechats* or cuts, united and fell again into their original places behind [the first three] and paused.'†

From this description it is clear that the couples divided to pass, each dancer singly, under one of the handkerchief arches (the middle man of the first three acting as the dividing pillar and holding the inside ends of both raised handkerchiefs) to cast off to right and left and so outside and down to the bottom of the set.

This was the dance performed in honour of James II when, on landing at Kinsale, he 'beheld with delight the dancing of the Fading'.

* Dinely: *Voyage through the Kingdom of Ireland*, 1681 (quoted by O'Keefe and O'Brian, *op. cit.*).

† J. Gamble: *A View of Society and Manners in the North of Ireland*, London, 1813.

[This communal string of dancers is precisely what occurs in the Faddy Dance at Helston, Cornwall, on May 8th, but here the string is double, for the dancers move in pairs. However, later descriptions show Irish dancers also in pairs, so what Dinely witnessed was perhaps some local variant. *General Editor.*]

The central figures of eighteenth-century Ireland, so far as dancing is concerned, were the dancing masters who travelled from place to place, usually having some other profession or trade in addition to that of teacher of dancing. Although little is known about them, it may be said that they were the creators of the step-dance. The dancing master was expected to be able to compose new steps, and it was as much by his powers in this direction as by his skill in dancing and teaching, that he achieved renown. The new steps went with him from town to town and were thus kept in circulation. One of the teachers of this period, O'Kearing, began to classify the various steps in use and helped to put them into the order in which they are found at present.

This process of invention of steps and their standardisation continued during the eighteenth and part of the nineteenth centuries. Thereafter came a decline, but it is certain that at least three great schools were in being about 1800—those of Kerry, Cork and Limerick. Since that period many of the dances had been forgotten and their revival was part of the broader Gaelic revival movement which began at the end of the nineteenth century.

✻ MODERN DEVELOPMENT ✻

Some dances are irretrievably lost, little remaining but their names, but the recovery of others and the revival of Irish dancing generally are due to the efforts of the Gaelic League (founded 1893) and is, in part, the revival of one of our oldest national functions—the *feis*.

The first *feis* was held at Tara long before the Christian era, when chieftains, druids, *fili* and *ollamhs* assembled to enjoy for three days the hospitality of the reigning monarch,

Plate 2   The Crimson Skirt worn as a Cloak. The Munster Cloak

after which they proceeded to the main business of the assembly, that of inspection of the National Records. Modern *feiseanna* embrace nearly all sections of Irish culture and are competitive; at the close of a *feis* it is customary to hold a concert in which the prizewinners of the various sections perform. The *Oireachtas*, a great national gathering, equivalent to the Welsh *Eisteddfod*, is held annually in Dublin. These gatherings have done much to standardise Irish dances, which are now classified in several well-defined groups.

THE DANCES

The terms group or *ceilidhe* are applied to the Round, Long and Square dances, the last-named usually the most difficult since their pattern is more varied.

Step, or solo, dances are the Jig, Reel, Hornpipe, the Slip or Hop Jig and a special class known as 'set dances'. These consist of measures composed to tunes such as St. Patrick's Day and The Blackbird, which do not conform to the regular structure of Jig and Reel tunes in that they are not composed of two parts with eight bars in each; St. Patrick's Day, for example, is comprised of 8–14 bars. The name is derived from the set piece or figure which is woven into each of them. Set dances are regarded as the highlight of solo dancing.

There are also some few dances called 'two-hand' because they are performed by couples, the couples progressing in the same direction round the room and performing the same steps simultaneously.

The origin of the Hornpipe is doubtful. Opinions differ as to whether it is English or Welsh; another suggestion being that the name originates from that of an instrument, the Irish *cornphiopa*, or hornpipe.

Perhaps the most distinctive characteristic of Irish dances, whether group or solo, is the neatness and precision demanded in their execution; to this must be allied a grace and agility without which their performance would become automatic. This does not mean that Irish dances are not performed in a carefree manner, but the spirit of gaiety is not allowed to interfere with the design of the dance or with the skill of the dancer. That spirit of gay abandon which sometimes pervades and enriches the folk dancing of other countries, has no place in Irish dancing where the performer is judged by the thoroughness and exactitude of his movements, whether in figure-work or in solo foot-work. A natural result of this emphasis on performance is that much of the dancing has become extremely intricate, although many of the older group-dances were simple in design.

In recent years, teachers have devised many new movements and designs and, in general, it may be said that these have embellished the dancing.

❧ MUSIC ❧

The music of Ireland has a long history. It is mentioned in the legendary tale of Tuatha De Danann, who kept a harper possessed of a magic harp, and of the chieftain who neglected to provide musicians and acrobats for the entertainment of his guests. Further references are found in the proto-histories of famous bards. The realm of history proper begins with St. Columba, the great Missionary Saint of the sixth century, whose Irish monks knew how to sing in counterpoint.

The harp is still the Celtic instrument *par excellence* not only in Ireland but in Wales, where the harpist, amongst other accomplishments, accompanies the unique Penillion singing, and in Scotland, where the Gaelic harp is so small that it must be raised on a stool. Only in Brittany are its strings no longer heard.

In more recent times the fiddle and the flute came into fashion and a tradition of country fiddling developed. It has become increasingly popular and now a class for the fiddle is included in many music competitions. Occasionally there is also a class for *Uileann* (elbow) pipes—for the bellows of the Irish pipes are tucked under the arm and blown by elbow movement. Their tone resembles that of the Northumbrian small pipes, less powerful than the great Scottish bagpipes.

Irish dance tunes developed, it is believed, from Clan and War Marches in quick tempo, often again quickened to 6/8 and 9/8 time for use as dance music. Today, combinations of fiddles, flutes, piano and drums are used for folk dancing.

The first serious attempt at collecting Irish airs was made by Edward Bunting (1773–1843). His life was devoted to this great work. The Belfast Harp Festival of 1792 supplied the final incentive: he not only gained the first prize for playing 'The Coolin', but there made friends with the many country harpers whose traditional tunes he afterwards wrote down.

The Irish Folk Song Society, founded curiously enough in London in 1904, as an offshoot of the Folk Song Society, preserved many of the lovely songs which were already beginning to fade from living memory. The Society's *Journal* containing these ran from 1904 to 1925 and was edited from 1920 by Donal O'Sullivan, who was responsible for publishing the Bunting Collection under the auspices of the Society. This great work has been all too little known.

Other collections are by Joyce, Petrie, O'Neill and Hughes, most of the tunes being noted from 'the singing of the people, the chanting of some poor ballad singer, the song of the emigrant, of the peasant girls while milking their cows . . . from the playing of wandering musicians or from the whistling of farmers and ploughmen'.

We are not very happy in the matter of costume, for the present 'traditional' costume as adopted by most dance schools seems to be neither traditional nor Irish, although it may be pleasing and distinctive in itself. However, there are quite a number of pieces of costume still being worn, such as the handsome patterned shawls seen in Connemara, the curiously worked belts worn by the men of Aran and the great black hooded cloaks of Munster.

Plate 4 shows a common eighteenth-century country dress, the girl with her shoulder shawls held in place by a laced red belt, her skirt tucked up and her long hair tied with a bow; the man in his short coat, breeches and stockings and a high-low hat. Unfortunately this costume has been travestied and defamed by its association with the stage Irishman, although it is an historic and traditional costume, appropriate to traditional dances.

It is known that the ancient Irish had a very beautiful costume and the present 'traditional costume' is the result of an attempt to reproduce this. The girls wear a sleeved, knee-length frock, usually adorned with Celtic embroidery, with a sash or braid at the waist and a short cloak, often attached by a Tara brooch at the left shoulder. A variety of colours are used. The men wear a saffron or green kilt with a short cloak hanging from the left shoulder, or shirt, trousers and sash. In fact, little has been discovered, as yet, regarding the ancient form of the women's dress, and with regard to the kilt, McClintock maintains that 'so far as the evidence here collected goes to show the sixteenth-century Irish dress did not include (1) the kilt; (2) a shoulder plaid or any such garment; (3) a sporran; (4) nor . . . a flat-topped cap like the Highland bonnet', and goes on to show that the Highland kilts did not evolve until long after the ancient Irish form of dress had fallen into disuse. There is much to be said for his suggestion that girls might adopt the costume worn in Ireland before the Famine: 'a crimson or other bright-coloured skirt with a bodice of black or some different colour, perhaps embroidered, and if needs be a shawl. . . . The crimson skirt indeed is of considerable antiquity in Ireland.'* It would be in keeping with tradition if a brighter attire were adopted, for many writers from the sixteenth century bear witness to the Irish predilection for bright colours.

WHEN DANCING MAY BE SEEN

Ceilidhes (organised dance gatherings) are held in nearly all the larger towns and in many country districts, normally under the auspices of some branch of the Gaelic League, the Gaelic Athletic Association or of a Folk Dance Society. These are usually advertised in the local press. At the larger gatherings it has become the custom to have exhibition dances performed by some noted team- or step-dancer, or both.

Feiseanna are held frequently in many parts of the country, and folk dancing may also be seen at annual Music Festivals in the larger towns of the North such as Portadown, Coleraine, Larne, Portstewart and Ballymena. These usually take place from February to September.

The Y.M.C.A., the Girl Guides and the Youth Hostels Associations have folk-dance sections.

The Gaelic League body, under whose auspices most of the *feiseanna* are held, is The Irish Dancing Commission, Parnell Square, Dublin.

* H. F. McClintock: *Irish and Highland Dress*, 1950.

THE DANCES

TECHNICAL EDITORS
MURIEL WEBSTER AND KATHLEEN P. TUCK

✺✺✺✺✺✺✺

ABBREVIATIONS
USED IN DESCRIPTION OF STEPS AND DANCES

r—right ⎫ referring to   R—right ⎫ describing turns or
l—left ⎭ hand, foot, etc.   L—left ⎭ ground pattern
C—clockwise   C-C—counter-clockwise

For descriptions of foot positions and explanations of any ballet terms the following books are suggested for reference:

A Primer of Classical Ballet (Cecchetti method). Cyril Beaumont.

First Steps (R.A.D.). Ruth French and Felix Demery.

The Ballet Lover's Pocket Book. Kay Ambrose.

Reference books for description of figures:

The Royal Scottish Country Dance Society's Publications. Many volumes, from Thornhill, Cairnmuir Road, Edinburgh 12.

The English Folk Dance and Song Society's Publications. Cecil Sharp House, 2 Regent's Park Road, London, N.W.1.

The Country Dance Book I–VI. Cecil J. Sharp. Novello & Co., London.

POISE OF THE BODY,
HAND GRASPS AND FORMATIONS

The poise of the body is upright but easy. The arms hang naturally to the sides unless otherwise described.

1 *Crossed Hand Grasp*

Dancers stand facing each other or side by side, r hand joined to r hand, l hand to l hand, the r hands being on top.

2 *Linked Arm Grasp*

Two dancers link arms with elbows bent and move round as described below in *Turn*.

3 *Advance and Retire*

Dancers hold inside hands and dance 2 Promenade Steps (see Basic Steps) forward and 2 backward.

4 *Turn or Swing*

Partners face each other r shoulders towards one another, both hands joined and move round C to complete a small circle.

5 *Right Hands Across*

a As in Rinnce Fada: The men of each set give r hands to diagonally opposite women. The four hands, in a wheel formation, are held above shoulder level and the dancers move C to places.

b As in The Ceilidhe, Four Hand Reel: The two men give r hands to one another, the two women doing the same, their hands being on top. Dancers move C to places.

6 *Swing Round*

This movement is a series of consecutive turns, usually danced by two couples. Partners join both hands and turn C at the same time progressing C-C round the other couple, both couples finishing in original positions.

	MUSIC *Beats*

Promenade Step. Count: Hop 1 and 2 (Jig or Reel time). This step to be used in all movements unless otherwise directed.

a Advancing

Hop on toe of l foot, the r leg stretched forward from the knee which is slightly bent, the toe pointing downward and outward. — and

Place r foot forward on ground. — 1

Close the toe of l foot to the near side of r heel. — and

Step forward on r foot, at the same time lifting l foot off the ground. — 2

Repeat hopping on r foot. — & 1 & 2

b Retiring

Hop on the toe of l foot. — and

Step well back on r foot. — 1

Close heel of l foot to toe of r foot. — and

Step back on r foot at the same time lifting l foot off the ground. — 2

Repeat hopping on r foot. — & 1 & 2

Rising Step or Rise and Grind (6/8 jig time—4 bars in all)

a The Rise Count: 1 and 2

Hop on l foot, raising r foot off the ground with the knee bent and then extended. — 1

Hop again on l foot, letting r foot swing backwards, without touching the ground. — and

Place r toe on ground at back of l heel. — 2

b The Grind Count: Hop 1 and a 2

Hop on toe of r foot, bringing l foot behind — and

r foot without letting it touch the ground.

Beat toe of l foot behind r heel.	1
Beat toe of r foot in front of l toe.	and
Beat toe of l foot behind r heel.	a
Beat toe of r foot in front of l toe.	2
Repeat the Rise and Grind beginning with hop on r foot.	1 & 2 & 1 & a2

Seven Step   Count: 1 and 2 and 3 and 4 (Jig or
  Reel time)

  Stand with weight on l foot, r foot forward
  with heel off ground.

Hop on l foot; land on the toes of both feet, the r heel covering the l toe.	1
Step a short distance to side with r foot.	and
Close l toe to r heel.	2
Repeat—step sideways on r foot and close l toe to r heel twice.	& 3 & 4

N.B.—1. Each step-close should be finished
with weight on l foot behind, the r foot raised
off the ground in front.

2. The women instead of jumping on the
1st beat of the step, usually dance a 'cut', i.e.
hop lightly on l foot at the same time drawing
the heel of r foot across the l leg below the knee.

Two Threes   Count: 1 and 2, 1 and 2 (Jig or
  Reel time). This step is danced more or less
  on the spot.

  Stand with weight on l foot and r foot forward.

Place r foot behind heel of l foot.	1
Place l foot a few inches to forward and to the L.	and
Close toe of r foot to heel of l foot.	2
Repeat bringing l foot behind.	1 & 2

Side Step   Seven Step followed by Two Threes
   (Jig or Reel time)

   The Seven Step is danced to R or L and is
   followed by the Two Threes. Should in-
   struction be given to repeat the step back to
   place or in the opposite direction it will be
   noted that the improper foot is forward.
   This foot will then have to be brought behind
   on beat 1.

All Side Step—partners passing

   When this direction is given and partners
   pass one another, those proceeding to their
   L pass in front. The woman will probably
   be going to her L first and so passes in front
   of her partner. On returning the man will
   be going to his L and so passes in front.

RINNCE FADA (*pronounced Rinky Fadha*)

Region Widespread.

Character An ancient dance of simple, pleasing movements.

Formation Longways dance for any even number of couples, men in one line and women in the opposite line. (O=woman, □=man):

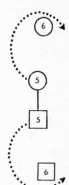

Dance	MUSIC
8 bars Introduction (A).	*Bars*
	A
1 Rising Step, hands joined in lines.	1–4
Right Hands Across in sets of two couples down the dance.	5–8
Repeat Rising Step and follow with Left Hands Across.	1–8

2*a* Odd couples join inside hands and lead down the middle. Partners release hands, and turn towards one another on 4th step.

They join inside hands, lead up to places and cast off one place behind the Even couple below them (see diagram).

b Odd men cross over to their own partners, while Even women cross to their partners and all dance Swing Round so that the two couples change places. All fall back to lines.

The dance is repeated. Odd couples dancing with the couple below them until they reach the bottom of the line. They remain neutral for one round of the dance and then move up the set as Even couples. The dance is repeated until all regain original places.

RINNCE FADA

Arranged by Arnold Foster

THE HAYMAKERS' JIG

Region   Widespread.

Character   A light-hearted dance.

Formation   Longways as in Rinnce Fada. (O=woman, □=man):

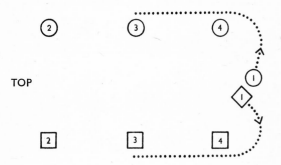

Dance	MUSIC
8 bars Introduction (**A**).	*Bars*
	A
1*a* Dance the Rising Step, hands joined in line. Advance and Retire in lines, hands still joined.	1–4 5–8
b 1st man and 4th, or last, woman advance to centre of the set, dance a full turn with r hands joined and return to places. 1st woman and 4th, or last, man do the same.	1–4 5–8

THE HAYMAKERS' JIG

Arranged by Arnold Foster

	B
1st man and 4th woman repeat, turning with l hands.	9–12
1st woman and 4th man do the same.	13–16
1st man and 4th woman repeat, turning with both hands.	9–12
1st woman and 4th man do the same.	13–16

	A
2 1st couple link r arms and make a full turn.	1–4
Dancers release arms, 1st woman and 2nd man turn with l arms linked while 1st man and 2nd woman do the same.	5–8
1st couple turn each other with r arms linked.	1–4
They turn 3rd couple as they turned 2nd couple.	5–8

	B
1st couple continue as above until they reach the bottom of the set.	9–16

3 1st couple cross over (the woman passing in front) and cast up on own side of the dance to the top of the set, the other dancers following their leader (see diagram).	9–12
1st couple meet at top, join inside hands and lead to the bottom of the set, the other dancers following. All fall back to lines with the 1st couple at the bottom.	13–16
Repeat with a new top couple until each dancer is back in place.	

N.B.—In each repetition of the dance the movements of Figure 1b are danced by the top and bottom couples in the set.

Plate 3   *Modern Dancer's Dress and the Tara Brooch*

THE CEILIDHE, FOUR HAND REEL

Region   Widespread.

Character   A set figure dance requiring a great deal of precision.

Formation   Two couples facing each other, women on the right of partners.

Dance	MUSIC
8 bars Introduction (A).	*Bars*

<table>
<tr><td>OPENING: LEAD ROUND</td><td>A</td></tr>
<tr><td>Partners join inside hands and both couples lead round a full circle C-C to places.</td><td>1–6</td></tr>
<tr><td>Release hands and make a half turn, turning inward towards each other.</td><td>7–8</td></tr>
<tr><td>Join hands again and lead round C to places.</td><td>1–6</td></tr>
<tr><td>Join both hands and turn to finish in places, i.e. both couples facing the centre, each woman on R of partner.</td><td>7–8</td></tr>
<tr><td>THE BODY (This consists of 5 movements A B C D E)</td><td></td></tr>
<tr><td>A The Square</td><td>B</td></tr>
<tr><td>In this movement each dancer performs 4 consecutive Side Steps along the 4 sides of the square, men moving to R, women to L.</td><td></td></tr>
<tr><td>Partners dance Side Step past each other (women passing in front) turning at the corner on the last bar of the step; men have r sides in line with 2nd side of square and women l sides.</td><td>9–12</td></tr>
<tr><td>All dance Side Step along 2nd side of square.</td><td>13–16</td></tr>
</table>

THE CEILIDHE, FOUR HAND REEL

Arranged by Arnold Foster

Continue in a like manner along the other 2 sides until all reach original places. | 9–16

B *The Sevens* | **A**

Partners dance the Seven Step past each other (women passing in front). | 1–2

Partners dance the Seven Step back to places (men passing in front). | 3–4

All repeat Seven Step across and back again. | 5–8

C *Right Hands Across* (See page 19) | 1–8

D *Down the Middle and Up the Sides* | **B**

Partners face each other: 1st couple join r hands and dance the Seven Step between the 2nd couple, who separate and dance the Seven Step on the outside. | 9–10

1st couple make a half turn and, releasing hands, partners dance back from one another, while 2nd couple meet and make a half turn with r hands joined. | 11–12

Repeat the movements of bars 9–12, the 2nd couple moving down the middle, the 1st couple on the outside. All finish in place. | 13–16

E *The Chain* | **B**

The men travel C, the women C-C.

All advance, give r hands to opposite dancers and change places, continue in square giving l hands to partners, r hands to opposite dancers and both hands to partners turning to original places. (2 Promenade Steps to each giving of hands.) | 9–16

FIGURE I: ADVANCE, RETIRE AND FIGURE EIGHT | **A**

a 1st couple join inside hands, advance towards 2nd couple and retire. (2nd couple stand a little apart.) | 1–4

1st couple turn with both hands joined.	5–8
1st couple dance towards 2nd couple, dancers release hands and 1st woman passes between 2nd couple then behind the 2nd woman, while her partner passes between 2nd couple and behind the 2nd man. The two dancers continue the figure-of-eight movement, the woman passing behind the 2nd man and the man behind the 2nd woman.	1–8
1st couple return to place and dance a full turn, giving both hands.	
	B
Both couples dance Swing Round.	9–16
b Repeat all movements as described in *a*, the 2nd couple performing the figure while 1st couple stand still, a little distance apart.	9–16 **A** 1–8 (twice)
THE BODY (i.e. A B C D E)	**B A B**
Repeat the whole of this part of the dance which is a chorus.	(48 bars)

FIGURE II: ARCH AND RING (O=woman, □=man)

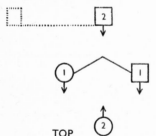

TOP

1st couple join inside hands to form an arch and advance to 2nd woman who dances under the arch.	**A** 1–2
1st woman, without releasing hands, passes in	3–4

33

front of her partner and together they make a
half turn to face 2nd woman who also dances
a half turn to her R. At the same time 2nd
man dances Side Step to R (see diagram).

1st couple and 2nd woman, joining hands to form a ring, dance Side Step to L, while 2nd man dances Side Step back to place.	5–8
The two women release hands to allow 2nd man to join ring and all dance Side Step to R.	1–4
Couples advance, 2nd couple passing under the arch made by 1st couple.	5–6
Partners make a half turn to finish in original positions.	7–8
Repeat Arch and Ring, 2nd couple making the arch.	B B

FINISH   A

Partners join inside hands and both couples Advance and Retire.	1–4
Repeat, finishing in a ring of 4 with hands joined at shoulder level and elbows bent.	5–8
All dance Side Step to L and back to R.	1–8

SIXTEEN HAND REEL

꘏꘏꘏꘏꘏꘏꘏꘏

Region	Widespread.
Character	A popular dance requiring good team work.
Formation	Circle of eight couples. (O=woman, □=man)
Dance	8 bars Introduction (A). Couples stand well spaced with 1 sides towards the centre, each woman on R of partner.

Couples, with inside hands joined, lead round
C-C to places.   1–8⎱
    1–6⎰

Partners turn with both hands to finish facing
centre (see diagram).   7–8

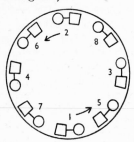

THE BODY (This consists of 3 movements A B C)

A *Side Step and Ring of Four*   **B**

All Side Step past partners, women passing in
front.   9–12

Repeat to places, men passing in front.   13–16

Couples 1 2 3 4 (see diagram) form rings of   9–16
4 by giving hands with couples on their R.
All Side Step to L and R finishing in places.

    A

Repeat above movement, couples 1 2 3 4 form-   1–8
ing the rings with couples on their L.   (twice)

B *The Half Chain* (women travel C, men C-C)   **B**

Partners face each other and move round the   9–16
circle giving alternately r and l hands to
each dancer they meet. On meeting partners
half way round, women turn inward to
finish on R of partners.

Partners take Crossed Hand grasp (see   9–16
page 19) and lead round C-C to places.

C *Link Arms and Swing Round* | **A**

The men of couples 1 2 3 4 move to R and linking r arms with men of couples 5 6 8 7 respectively, make a full turn. | 1–4

They turn the women of the same couples with l arms. | 5–8

Each man returns to place, passing r shoulder with the man he first danced with, and turns his own partner with r arm. | 1–4

Couples of each set of 4 (e.g. 1 & 5, 2 & 6, 3 & 8, 4 & 7, Swing Round each other to places. | 5–8

FIGURE I: ADVANCE, RETIRE AND SWING ROUND (This movement is performed by 1st and 2nd couples alone.) | **B**

Couples 1 & 2 Advance and Retire, inside hands joined. | 9–12

Repeat. | 13–16

Couples 1 & 2 Swing Round each other. | 9–16

This Figure is repeated by all the other couples in the following order: 3 & 4, 5 & 6, 7 & 8. | **A B A**

THE BODY

Repeat movements A B C. | **B A B A**

FIGURE II: MEN VISIT THE OPPOSITE WOMEN | **B**

1st and 2nd men cross over and turn opposite women with r hands. | 9–12

Men pass r shoulders and turn own partners by l hands. | 13–16

1st and 2nd men meet in centre, link r arms and make a full turn; they cross to opposite women and turn with l hands; they return to own partners and join both hands. | 9–16

SIXTEEN HAND REEL

Arranged by Arnold Foster

Couples 1 & 2 Swing Round each other.
This Figure is repeated by all the other couples in the order described in Figure I.

1-8
1-8
B A B

THE BODY

Repeat movements A B C.

A B A B

FIGURE III: ARCH AND SWING ROUND

A

TOP

(○=woman, □=man)

a 1st and 2nd couples advance to the centre with inside hands joined, 1st couple making an arch.

1-2

2nd woman moves under the arch and forward while her partner dances the Two Threes on the spot and the 1st couple make half a turn with both hands joined to face 2nd man.

3-4

2nd man now passes under the arch to join his partner. The 1st couple dance forward as they make the arch (see diagram).

5-6

Couples 1 & 2 turn with both hands in opposite places.

7-8

b Repeat the movements of III*a*, 2nd couple making the arch. All finish in original places.

1-8

Plate 4   *Eighteenth-century Costumes*

Couples Swing Round each other finishing in places.	B
	9–16
Repeat in order described in Figure I, couples 3, 5 & 7 making the arches first.	B (once)
	A B A B

FINISH: ALL TO THE CENTRE	A
All join hands and advance towards the centre and retire.	1–4
Repeat.	5–8
Retaining hands, dance the Side Step to R and back to L.	1–8
	B
Repeat Advance and Retire twice.	9–16
All Side Step to L and back to R.	9–16

N.B.—When advancing, confine the space of the step and let the hands sway smoothly down and then raise gradually to head level on reaching the centre. When retiring let the hands sway down and as the circle expands raise them to shoulder level.

BIBLIOGRAPHY

FLOOD, and GRATTAN, W. H.—*History of Irish Music.* Dublin, 1905.

GRAVES, P.—*Celtic Song Book.* London, 1928.

JOYCE, P. W.—*Social History of Ancient Ireland.* London, 1903.

MCCLINTOCK, H. F.—*Old Irish and Highland Dress.* Dundalk, 1950.

O'CURRY, E.—*Manners and Customs of the Ancient Irish.* London, 1873.

O'KEEFE, J. G. and O'BRIAN, A.—*Handbook of Irish Dance.* Dublin, 1902.

O'RAFFERTY, PEADAR.—*The Irish Folk Dance Book* (2 vols.). London, 1934 and 1950.

O'SULLIVAN, DONAL.—*Irish Folk Music and Song.* Colm O'Lochlainn, Dublin, 1952.

——(Editor) *The Bunting Collection.* Journal of the Irish Folk Song Society. Volumes XXII–XXIX, 1927–39.

SHEEHAN, J. J.—*A Guide to Irish Dancing.* London, 1902.

WEBB, A.—*Compendium of Irish Biography.* Dublin, 1878.